THIS BOOK BELONGS TO:

____

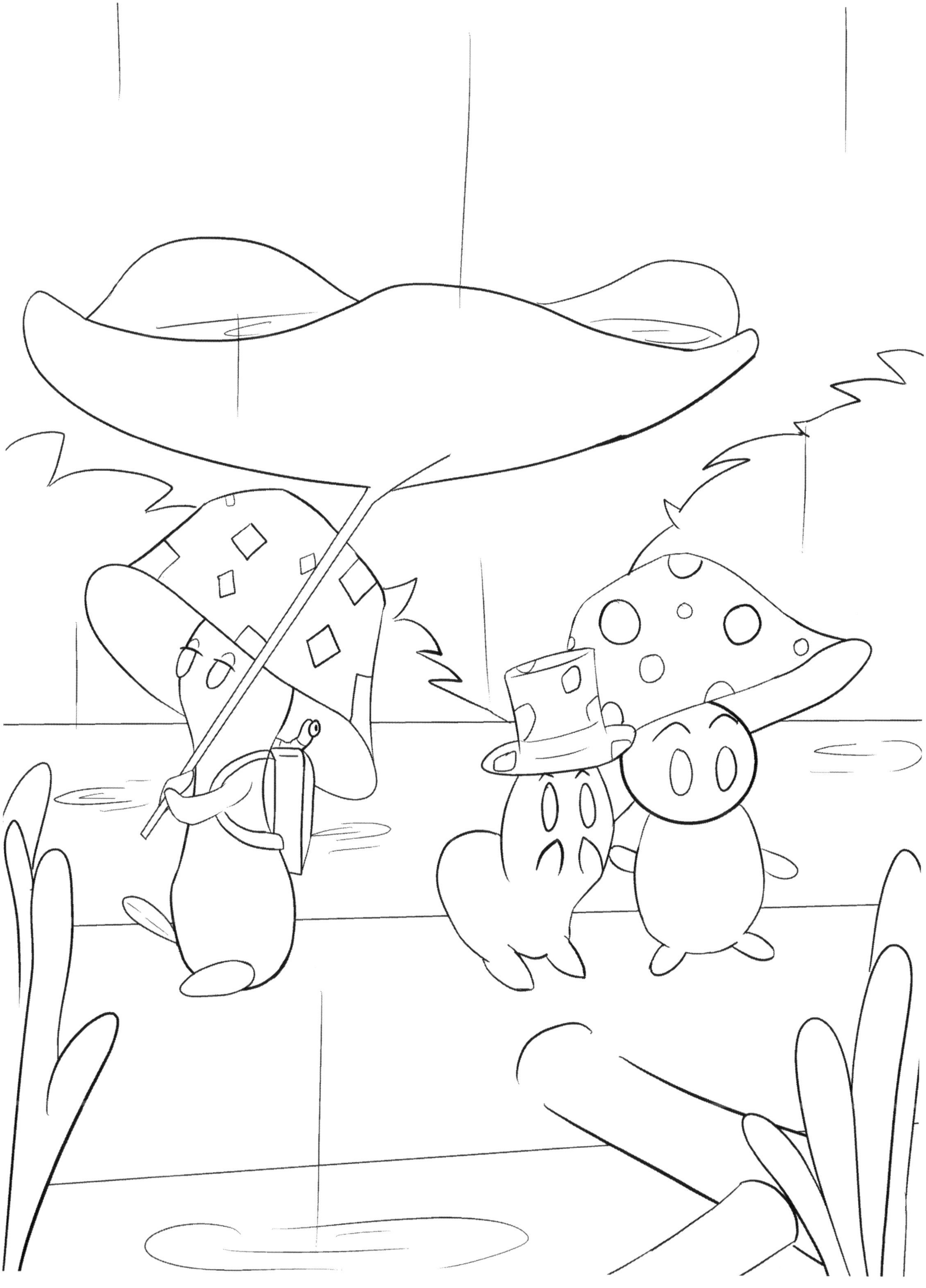

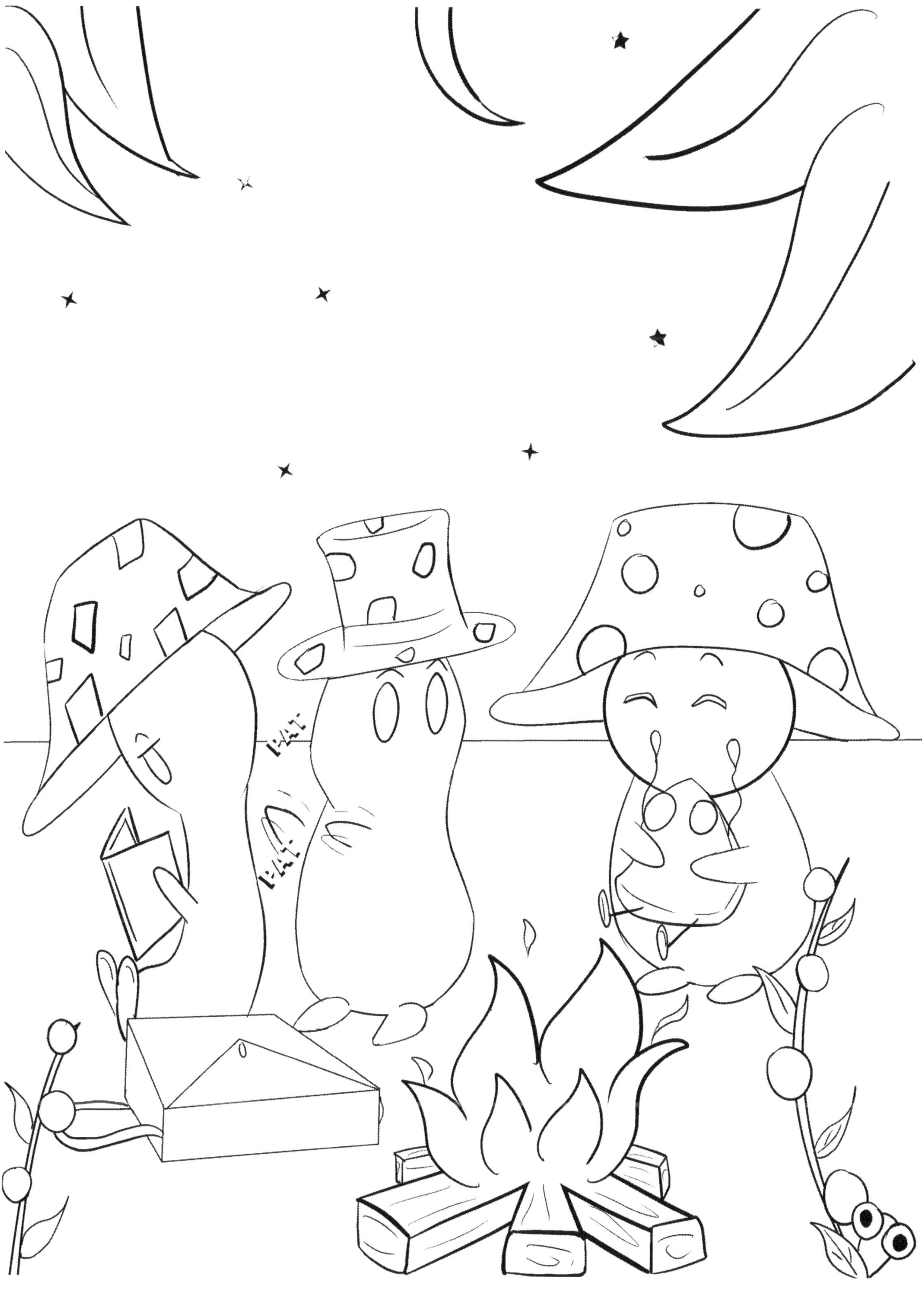
PAT
PAT

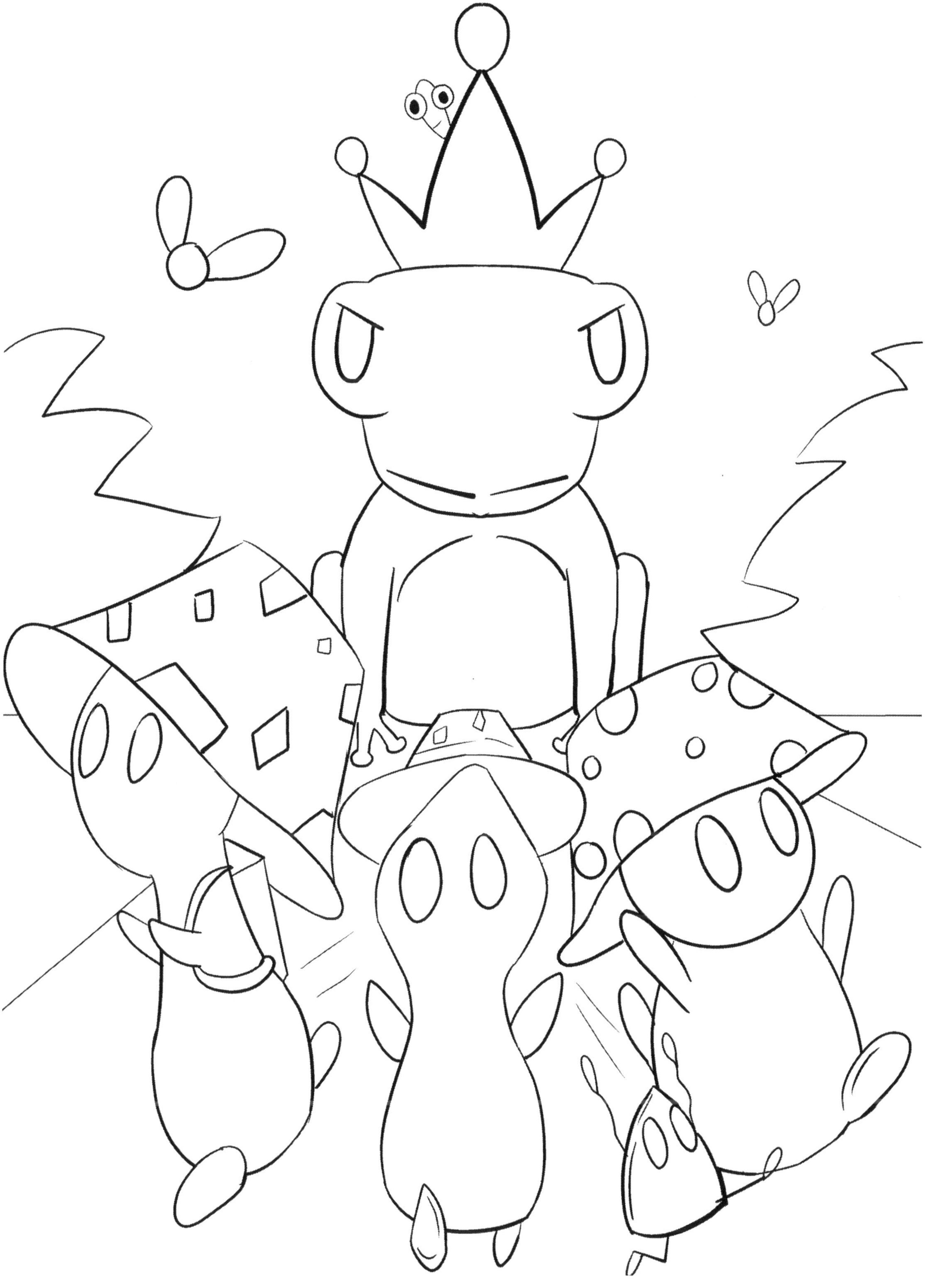

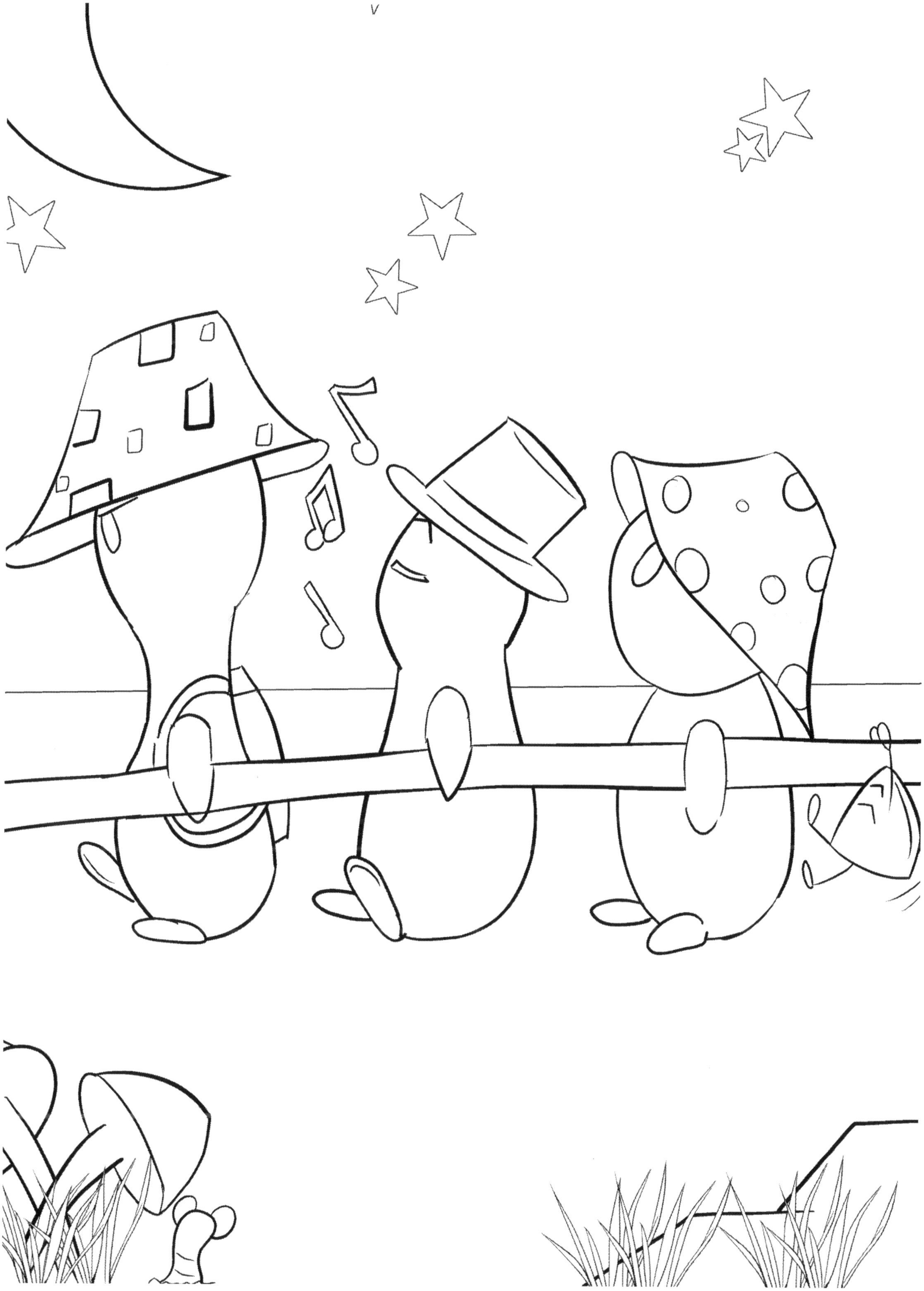

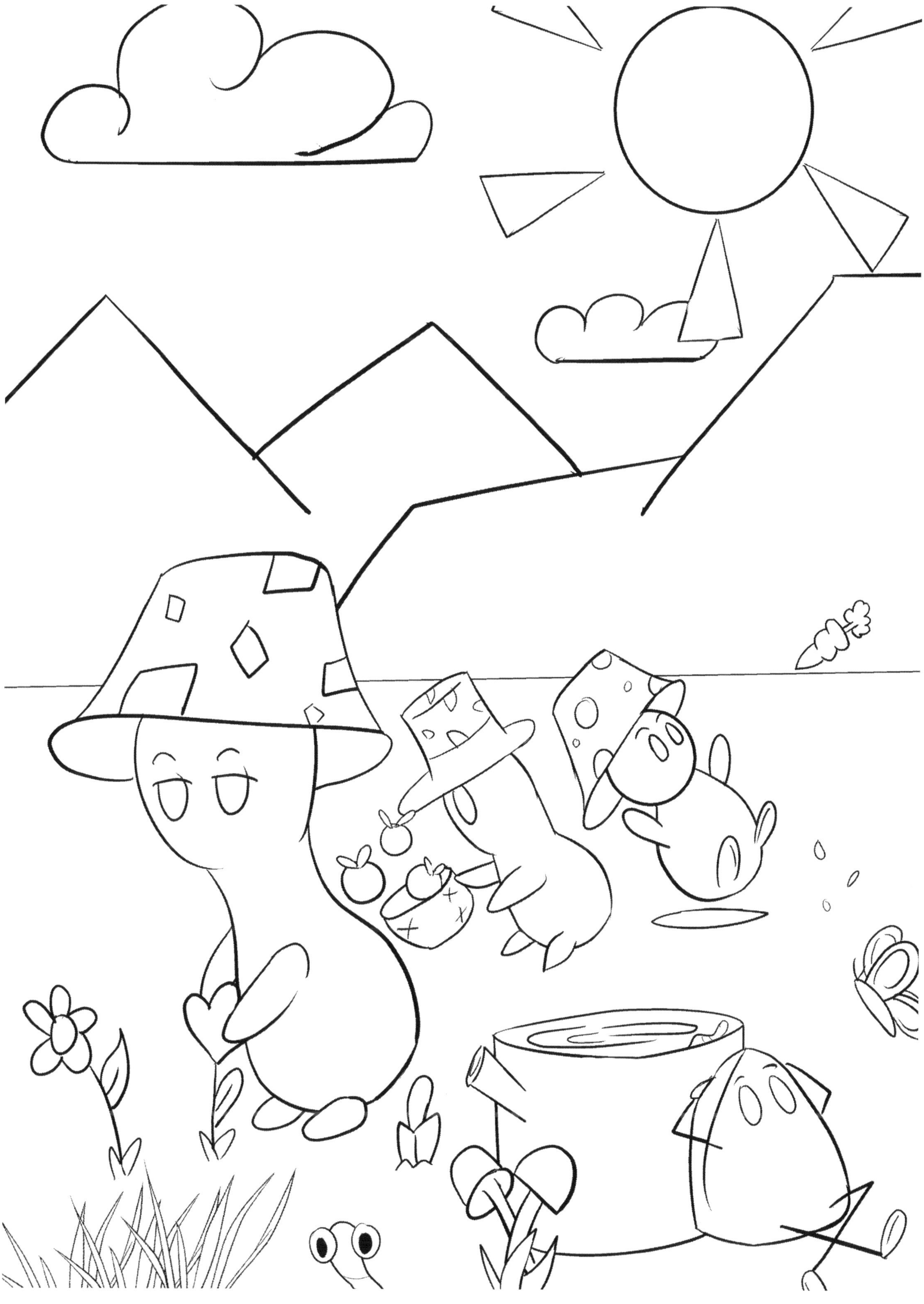

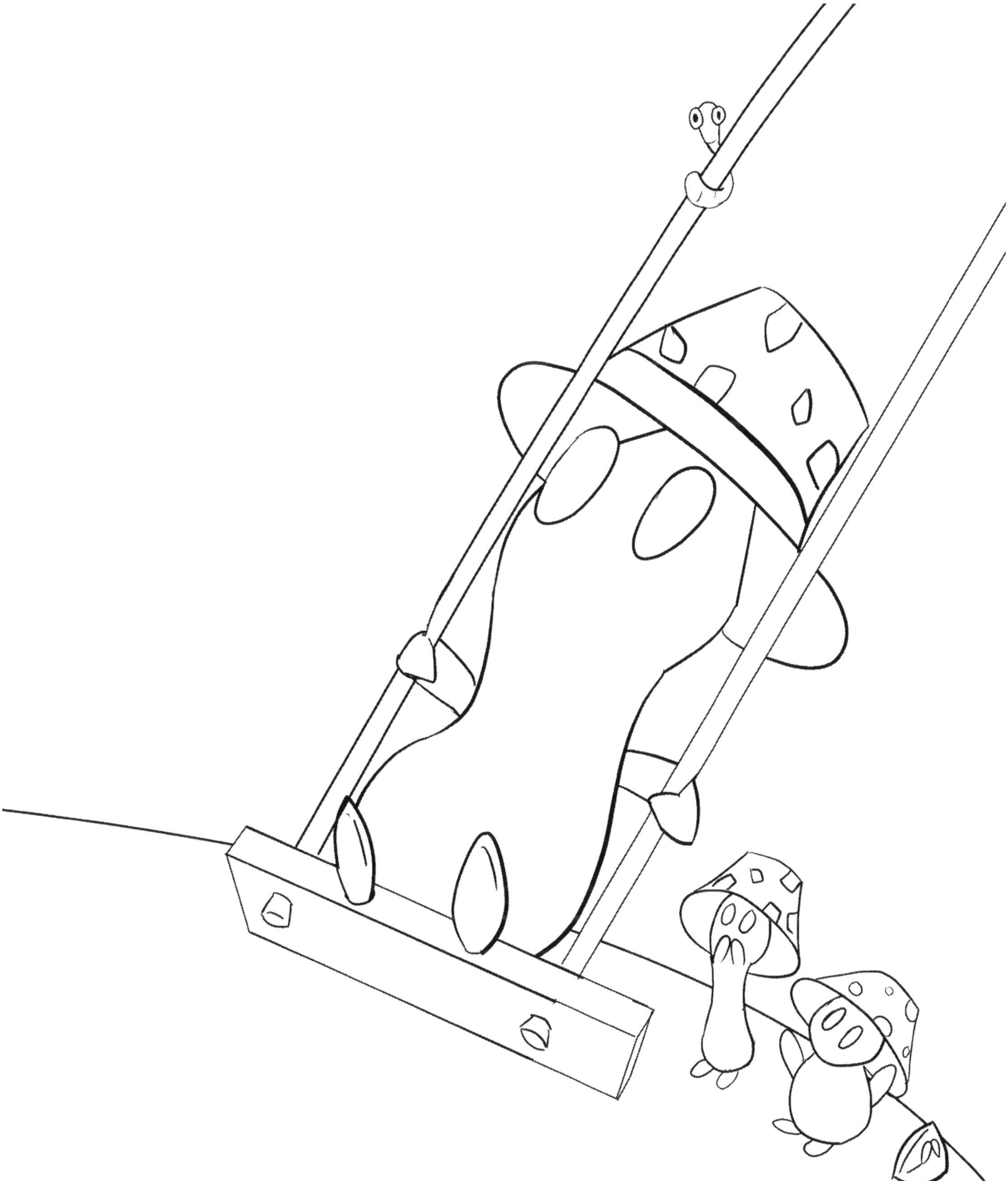

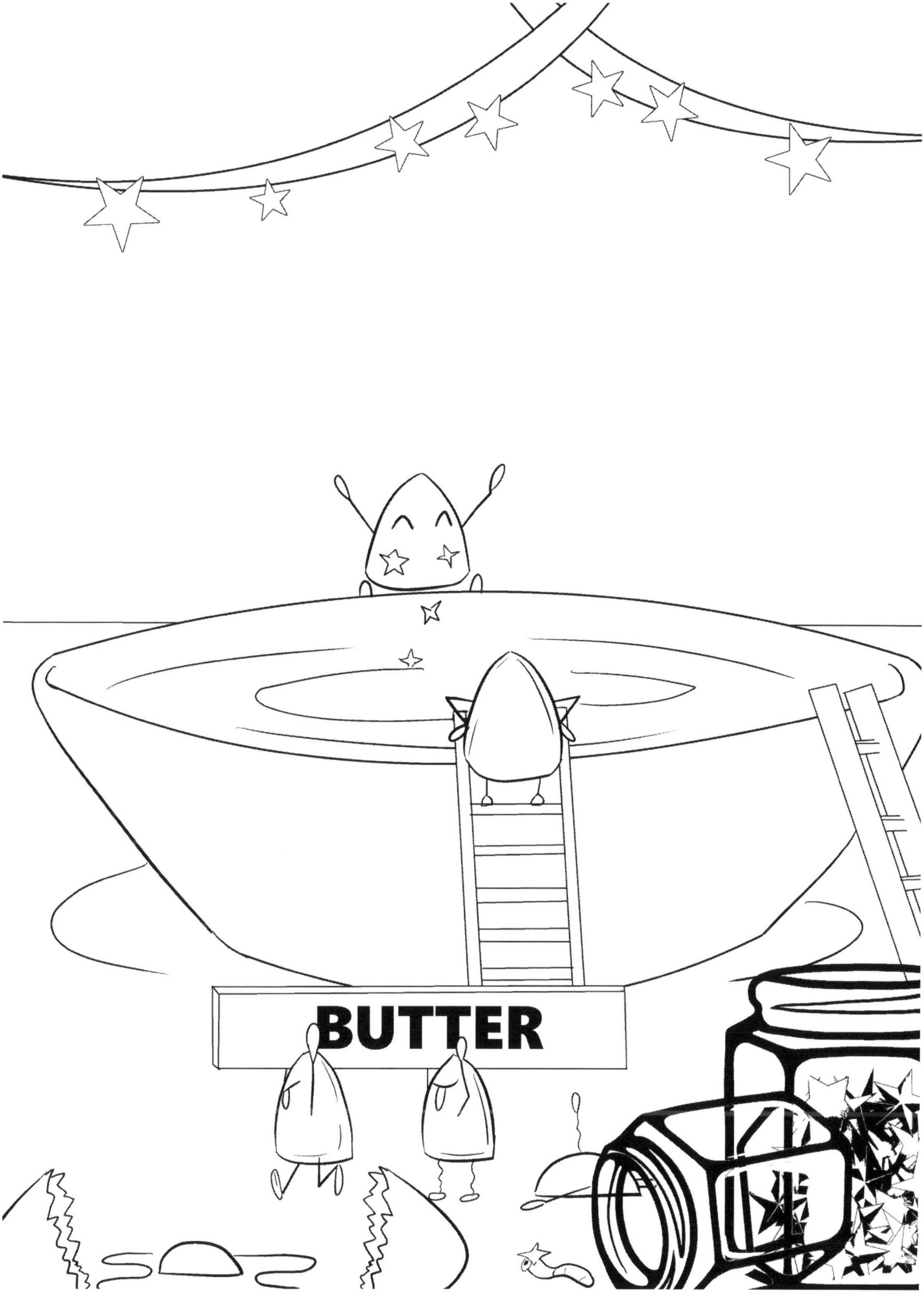
BUTTER

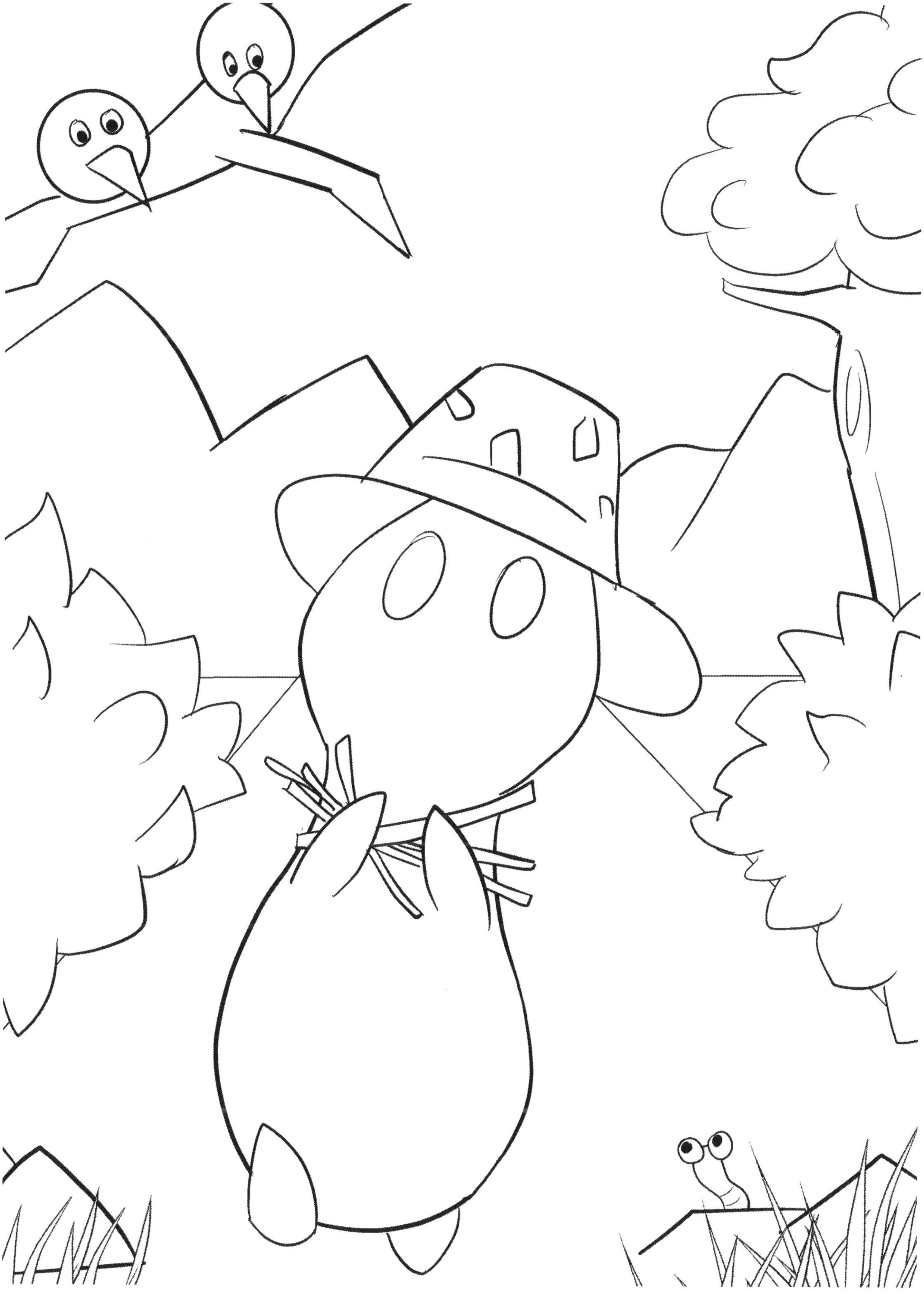

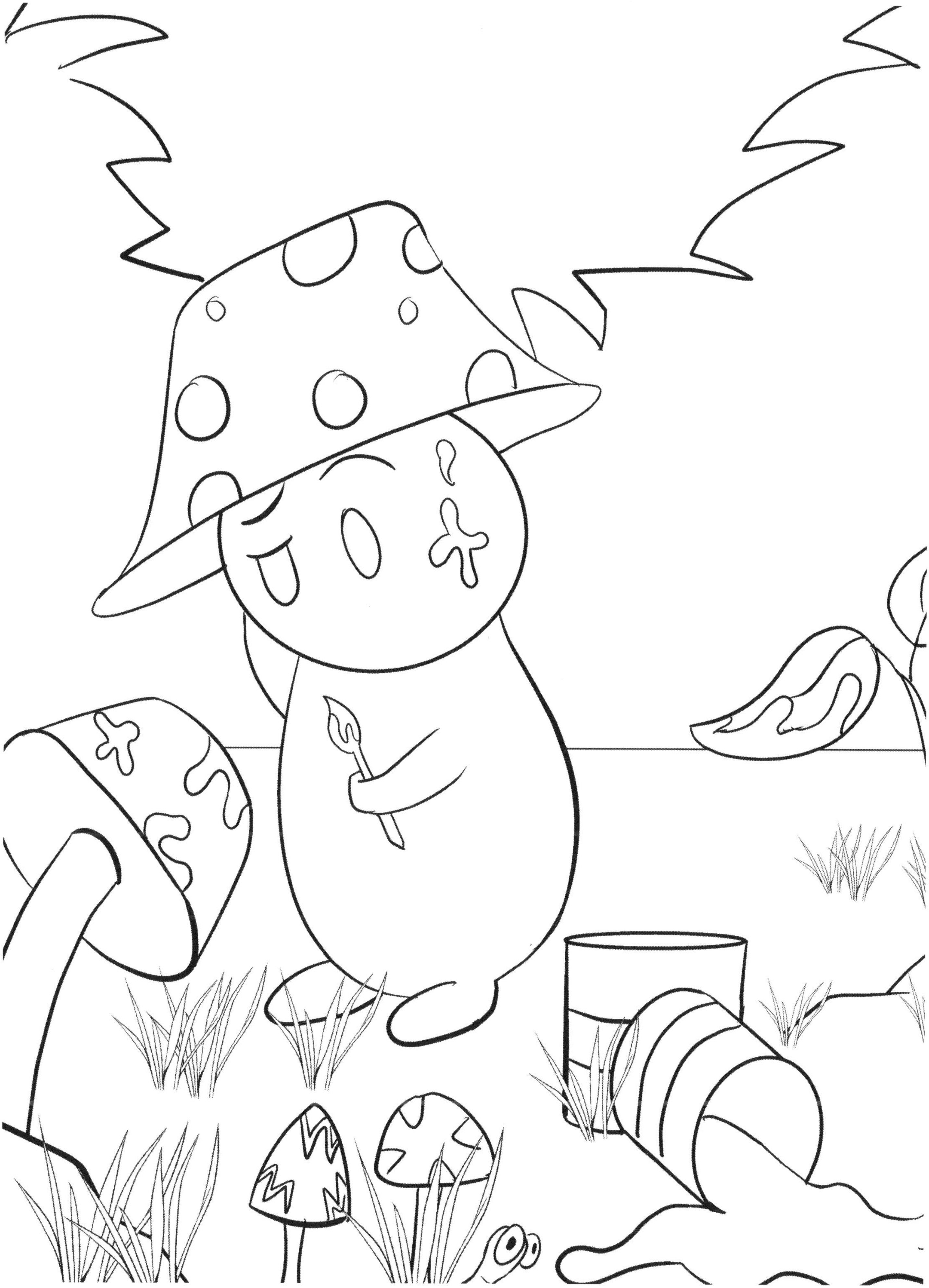

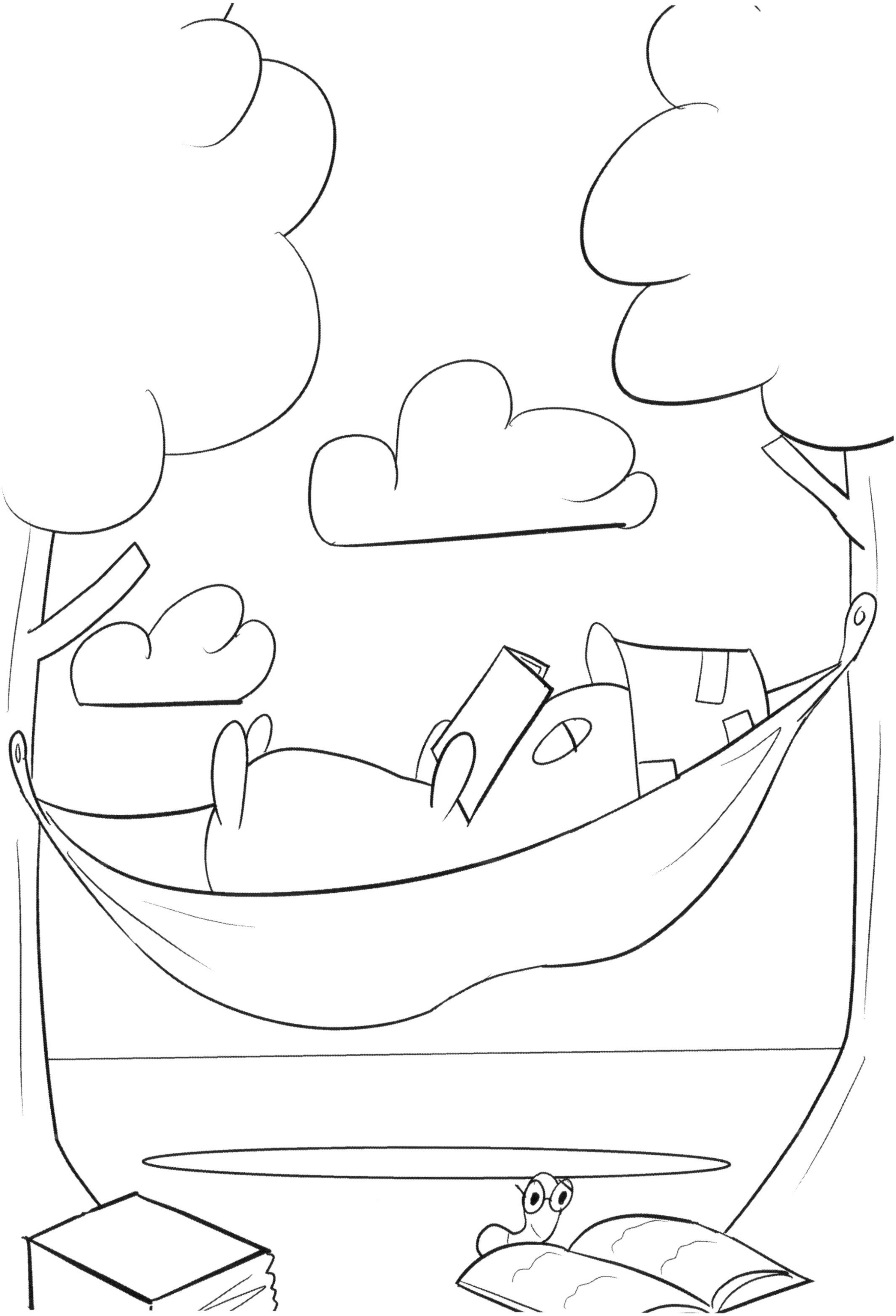

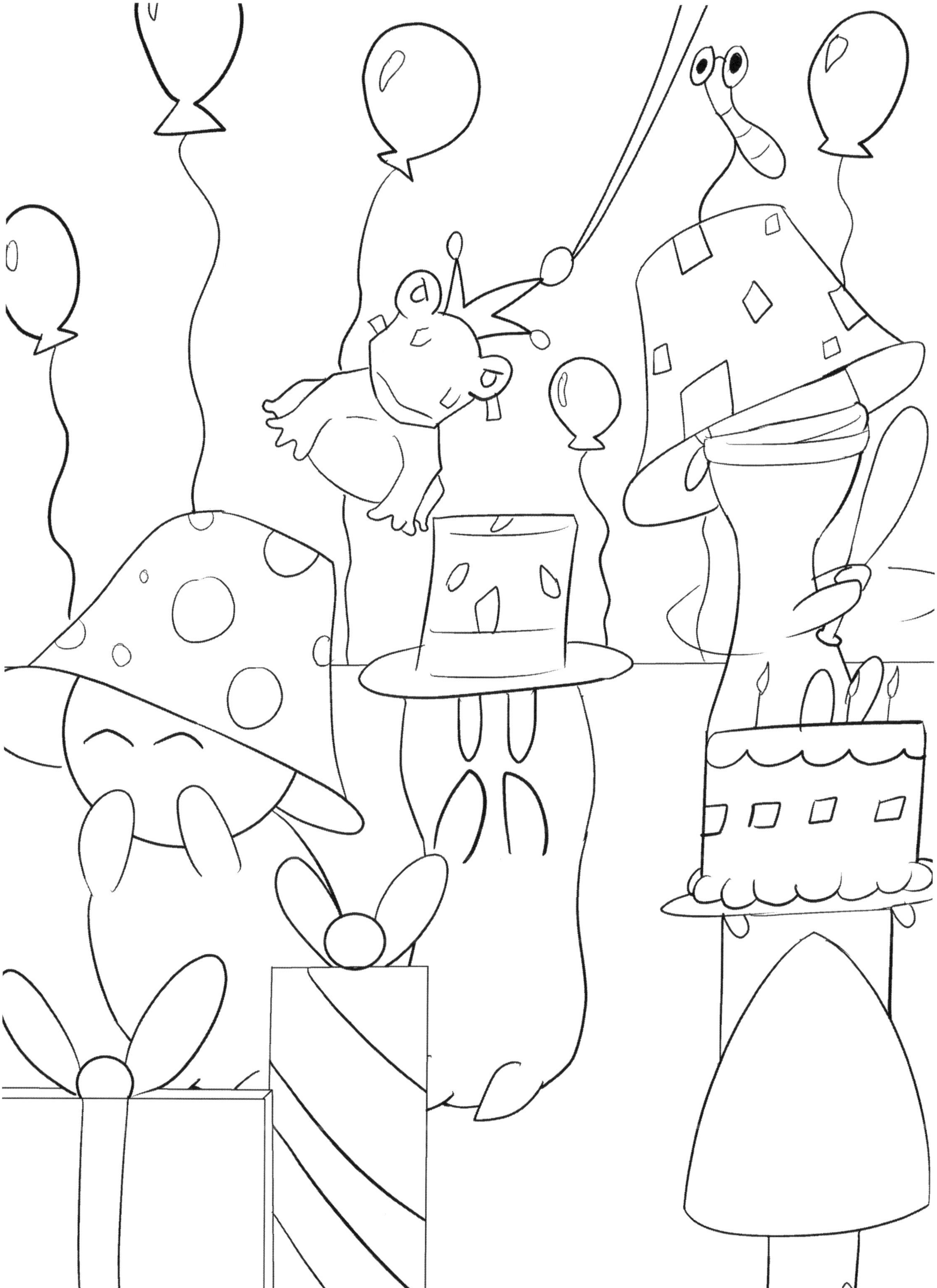

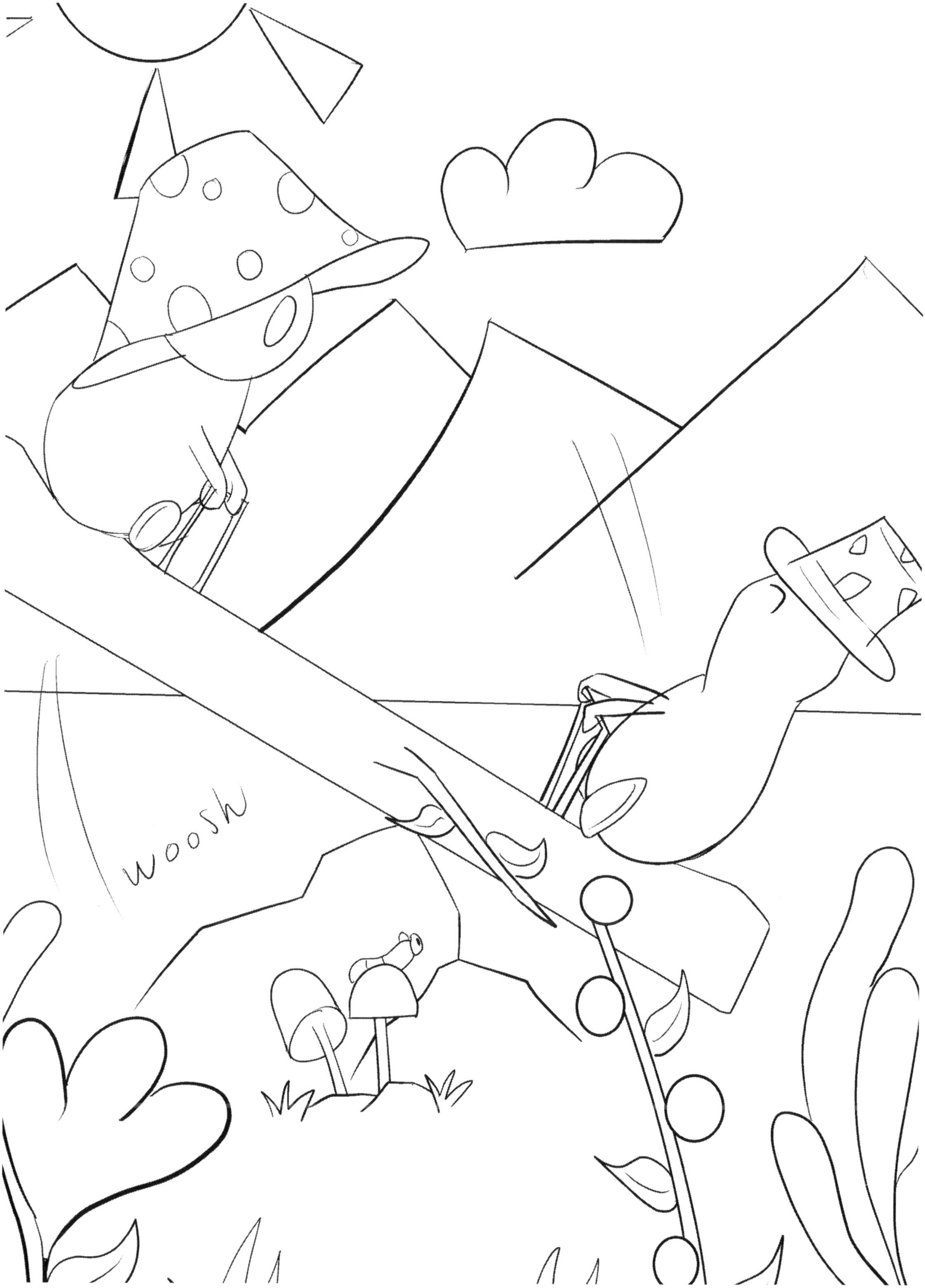
woosh

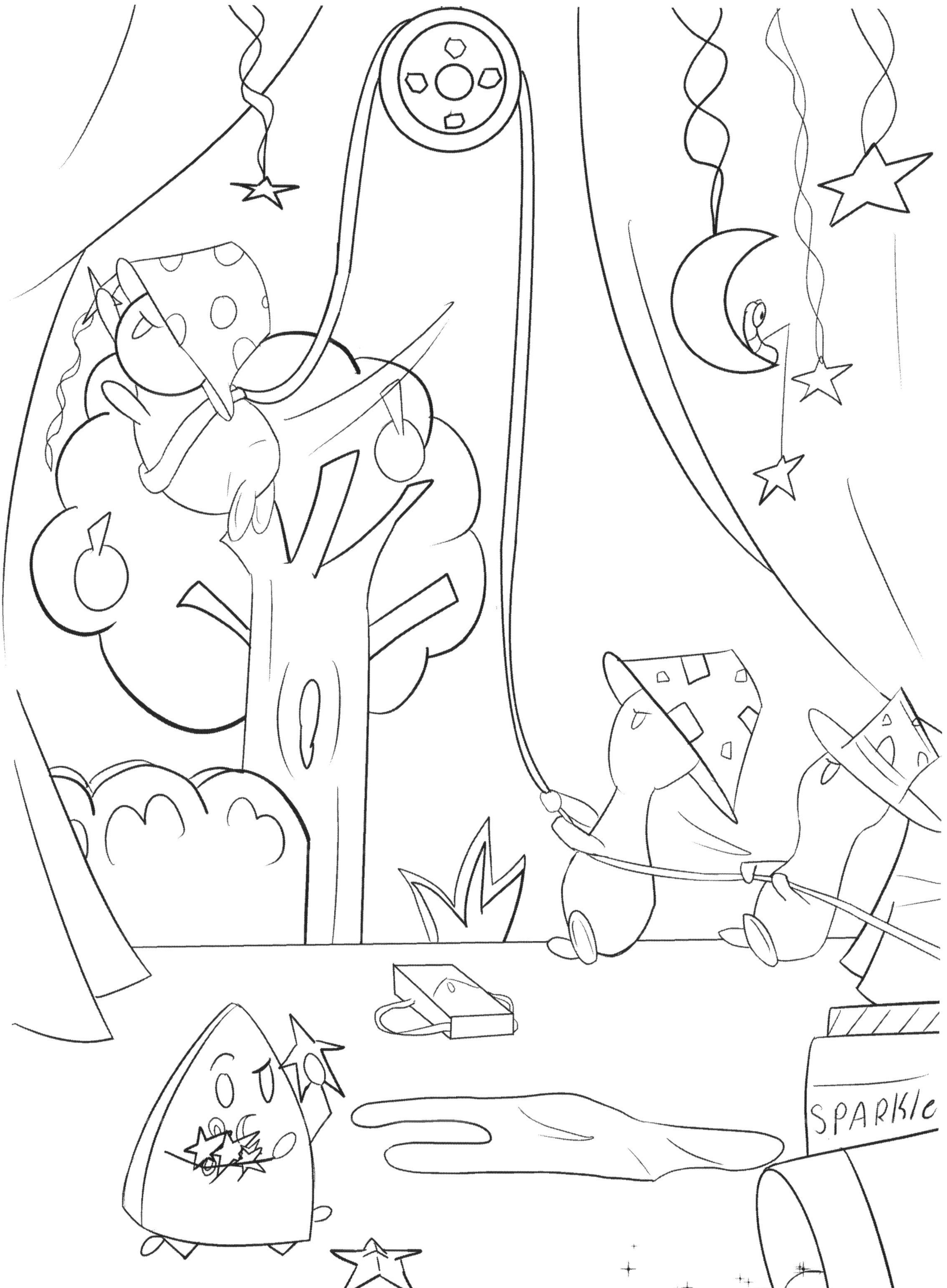
SPARKle

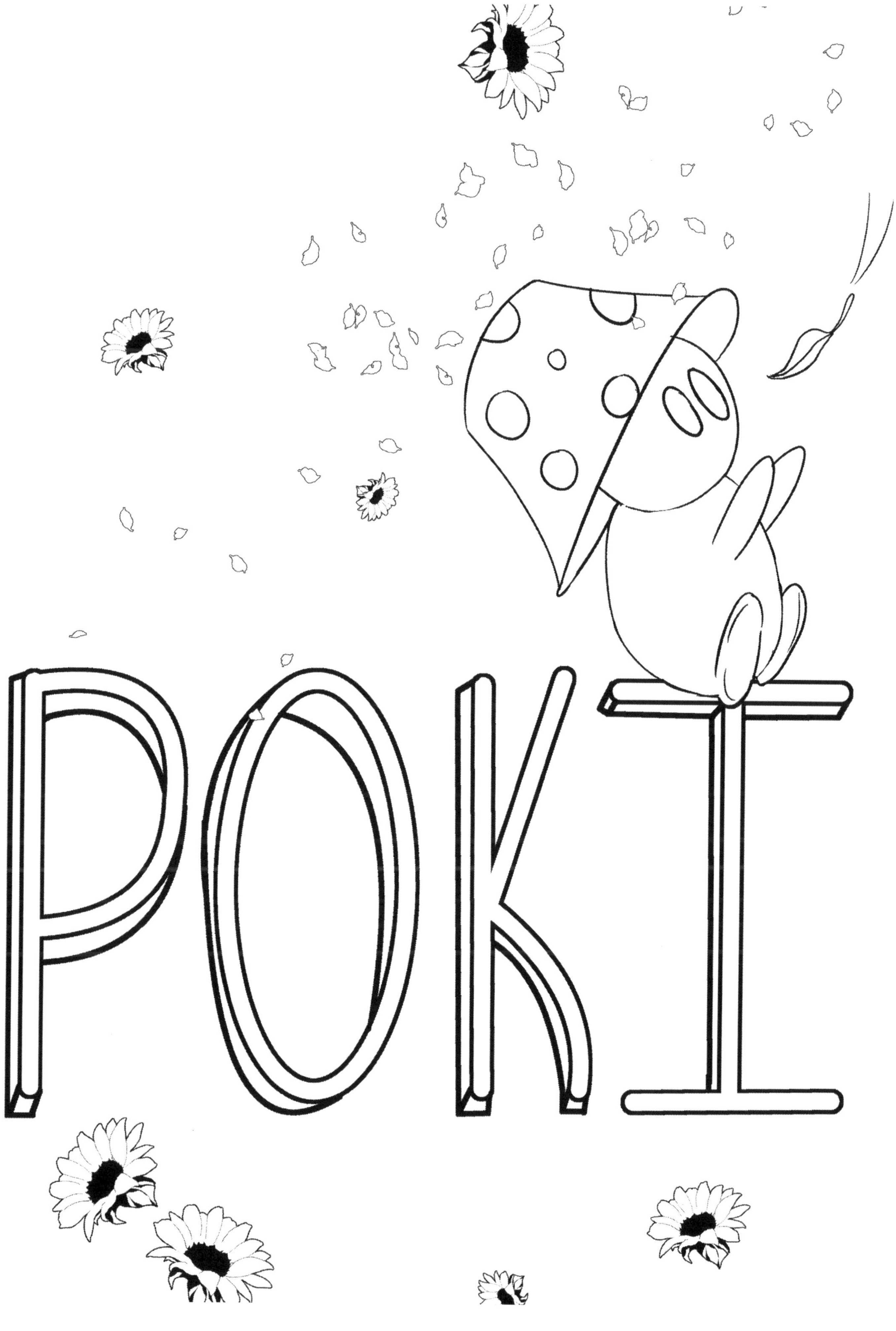
POKI

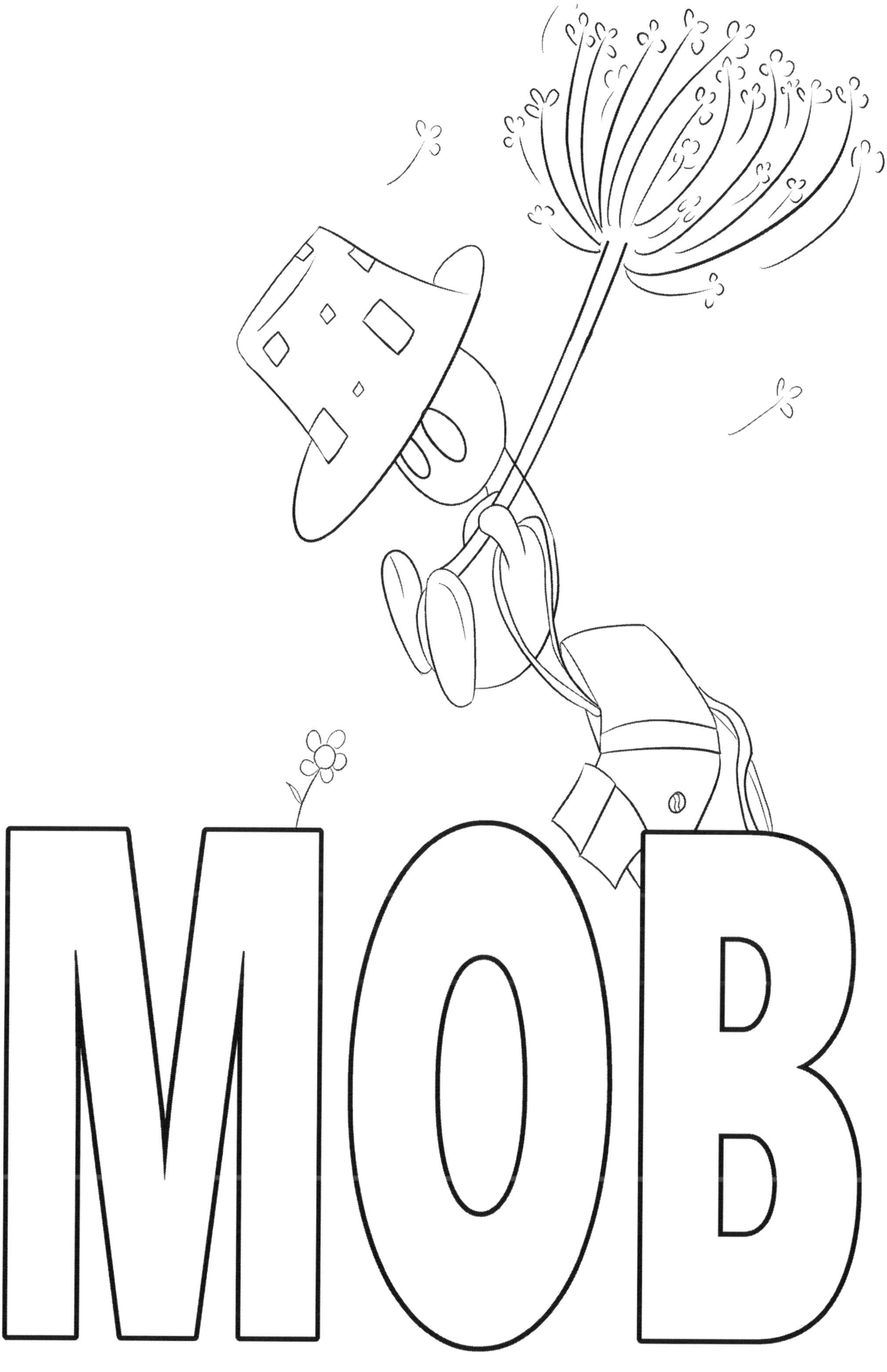
MOB

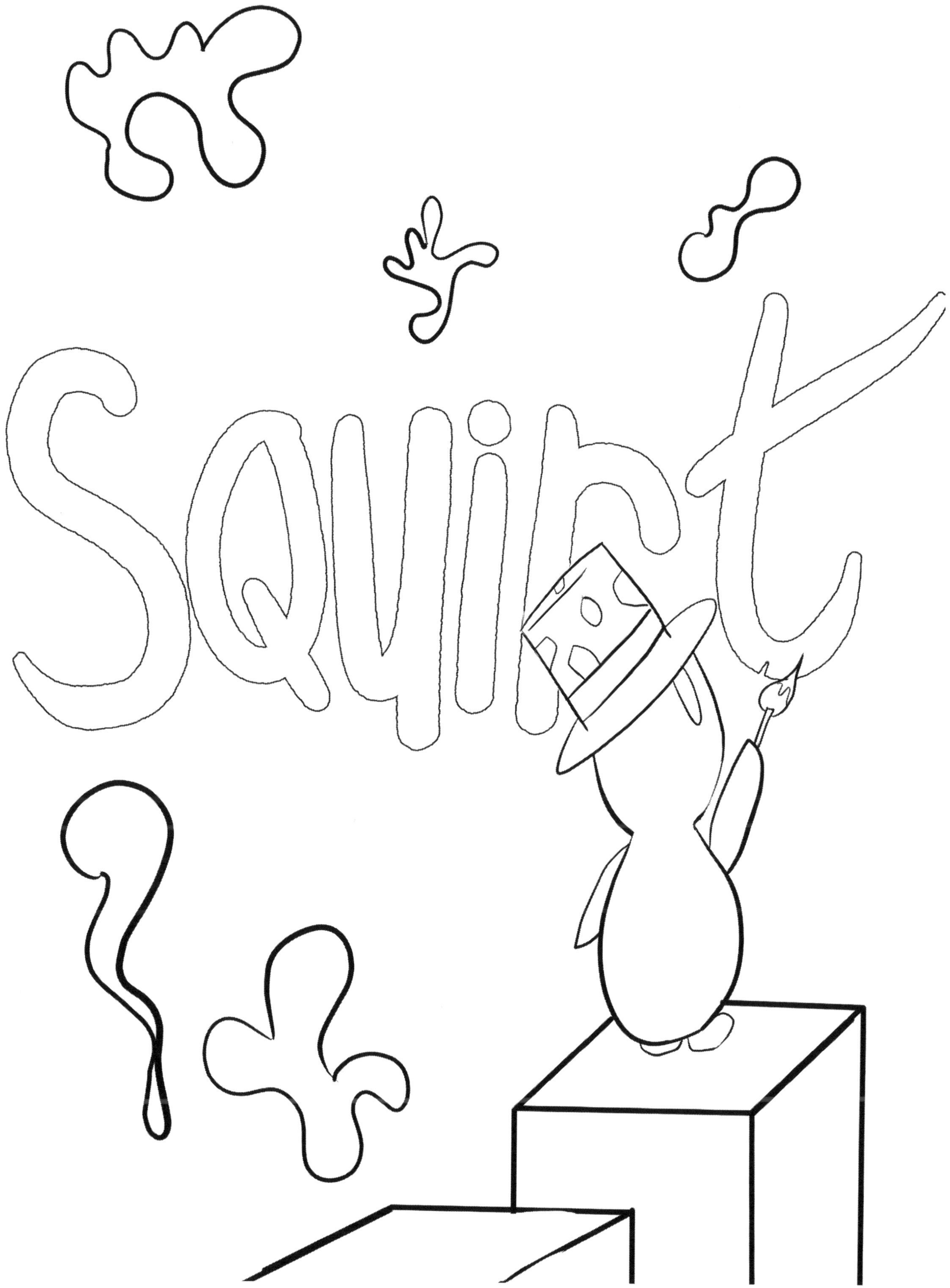
Squirt

CHIPS

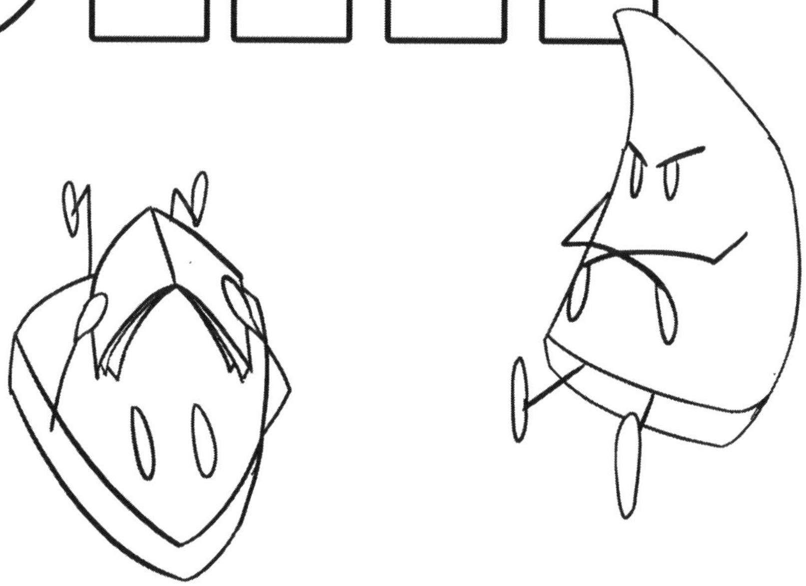

MARTIN

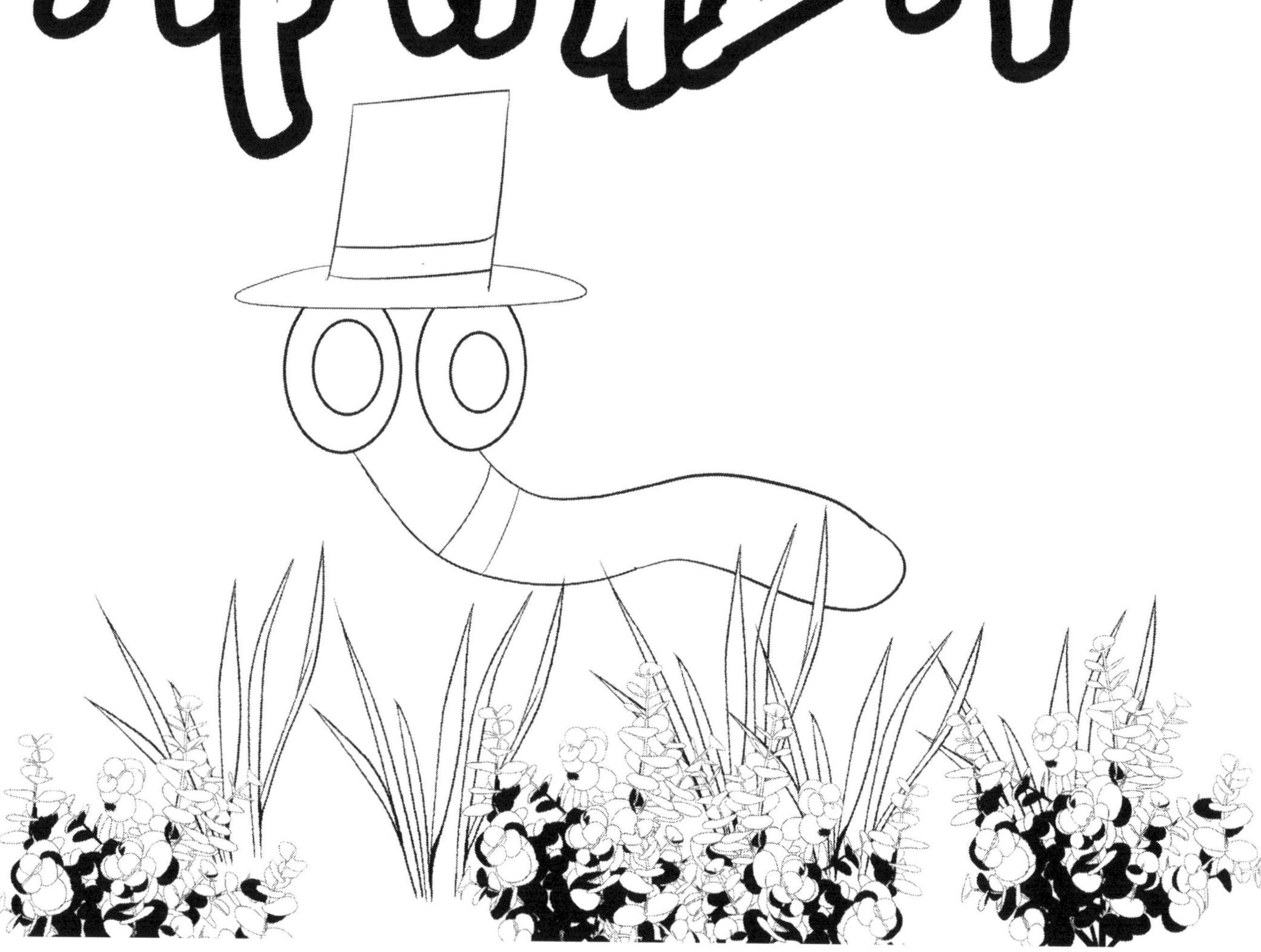

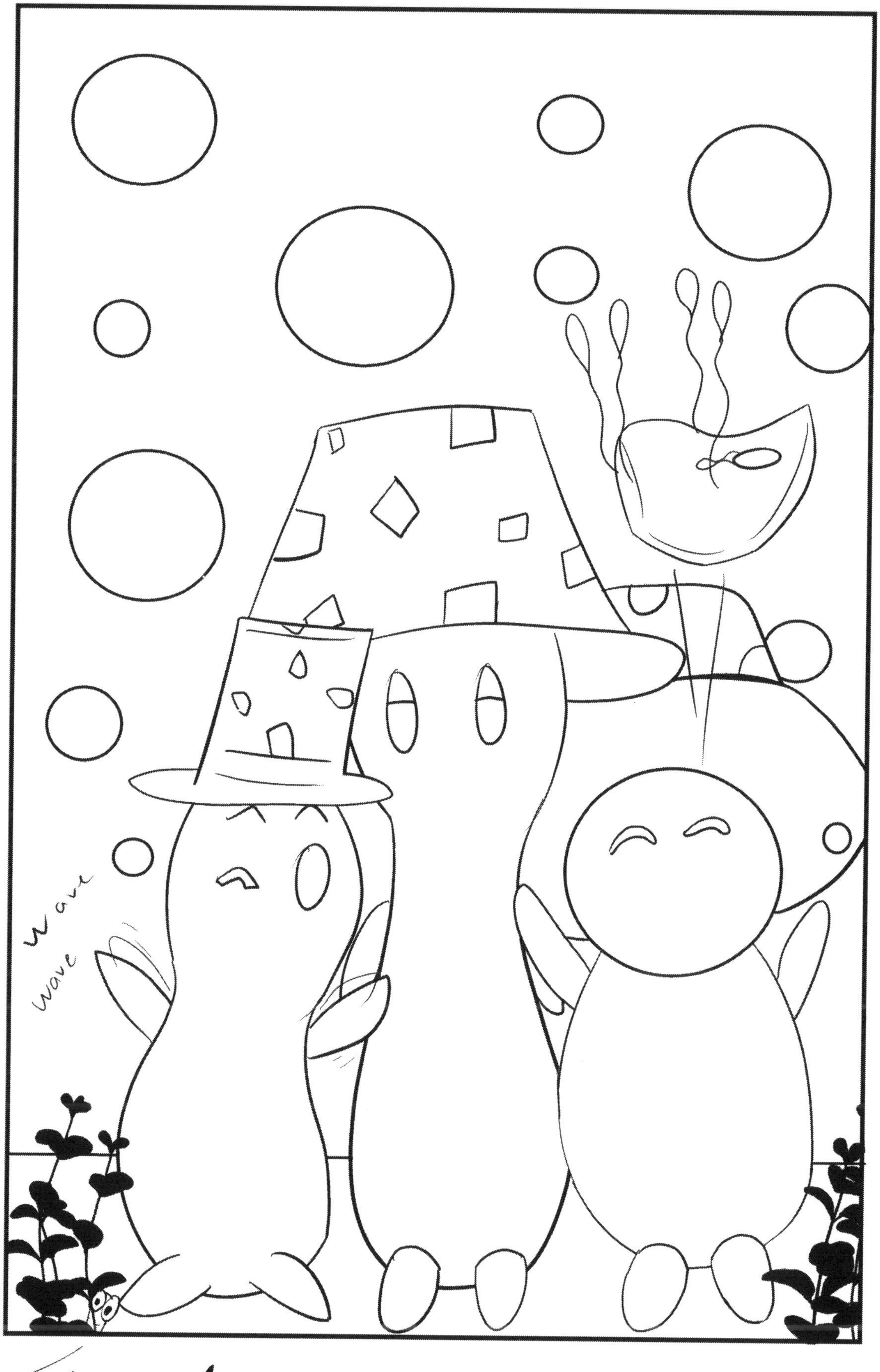

Thankyou for this fun Adventure

Made in the USA
Monee, IL
07 November 2024

69612558R00024